PHOTOGRAPHS **Chris Hill**

TEXT **Colin McCadden**

*The Province
of Ulster*

BOOKLINK
SCENIC IRELAND

ULSTER

Cúige Uladh

The province of Ulster comprises nine of Ireland's 32 counties. Our tour begins in Antrim and travels westward through Londonderry and Donegal, continuing into Tyrone, Fermanagh, Cavan, Monaghan and Armagh before ending in county Down.

A brief outline of Ulster's history, by far the most complex of Ireland's provinces, will provide a context within which to understand its geography, politics and religion.

Earliest records of the province begin before the time of the written word, and survive in such ancient legends as 'The Ulster Cycle' which features one of Ireland's most famous heroes, Cúchulainn, 'The Hound of Ulster'. As these records show, Ireland's most northerly province has witnessed many periods of territorial and political conflict.

The O'Neill dynasty, descendants of the Irish Royal family of Tara, were kings of Ulster and monarchs of all Ireland from as early as the 5th century until the 17th. It was in 1601 that Hugh O'Neill, the last great leader of Gaelic Ireland, was defeated by the English in a battle which marked the finale in England's long-suffering efforts to conquer Ireland. The terms of surrender granted to the rebels had a principal condition stating that lands formerly contested by feudal right and Gaelic law would, from that time on, be held under English law.

What followed in Ulster formed the basis for the cultural clash that continues to cause conflict to this day. In 1607, under the monarchy of James I, a planned process of colonisation settled English-speaking Scottish and English Protestants on Ulster lands that had been confiscated from Gaelic Catholic landowners. This 'Plantation of Ulster' was designed to prevent any further rebellion in what had revealed itself in the preceding century to be the province most resistant to English invasion. But despite the 'Plantation', rebellion proved to be inevitable and Ulster became a

Late evening light on
the Giant's Causeway,
the undisputed jewel in
Ulster's crown

Lava from a volcanic eruption
cooled slowly to form this
unique collection of polygonal,
basalt columns on Ulster's
north coast.

bloody battleground for nearly forty years, a situation only resolved
(temporarily) with the defeat of the Irish Catholics and the occupation
of the province by Oliver Cromwell's army.

By the late 1600s, the struggle for British power became all the
more fraught with the staunch Roman Catholic, James II, on the
throne. Many of his subjects distrusted his religious policies, leading a
group of them to depose him. He was replaced, not by his Roman
Catholic son, but by his Protestant son-in-law, William III, and
daughter, Mary II, who became joint rulers in 1689.

James made one serious attempt to recover his throne when he
landed in Ireland in late 1689. But in 1690, despite having the
support of the native Irish Catholics, he was defeated by William and
his army of Protestant settlers at the Battle of the Boyne near
Drogheda in County Louth.

William's victory ensured British and Protestant supremacy in
Ireland for over a hundred years, but this inevitably left the country
facing conflict, not only between Ireland and Britain but also between
Catholic and Protestant. By the 20th century, when Home Rule was
finally granted, most of the former Gaelic stronghold of Ulster, now
predominately Protestant and firmly loyal to Britain, objected.

Only three of Ulster's counties had a majority in favour of Home
Rule, leaving six that wanted to remain allied to Britain. The ensuing
Government of Ireland Act (1920) defined the six counties of Antrim,
Armagh, Down, Fermanagh, Londonderry (formerly Coleraine) and
Tyrone as Northern Ireland, an administrative division of the newly
formed 'United Kingdom of Great Britain and Northern Ireland', with
Cavan, Donegal and Monaghan becoming part of 'Southern Ireland',
or the Free State, now the Republic of Ireland. Effectively then, the
province of Ulster encompasses two different countries, yet maintains
its status as one of the 'four proud provinces of Ireland'.

Setting historical and political complexities aside, the photographs
in this book are intended to draw attention to the scenery and major
points of interest the province has to offer – and Ulster has more than
its fair share. In an area of nearly 9,000 square miles (just over 24,000
square kilometres), it boasts a variety of hills, lakes, glens, mountains
and boglands, dressed in purple heather in the summer and wind-dried
grasses in autumn.

The counties of Down, Antrim, Derry and Donegal are bounded to
the east, north and west by some 400 miles of coastline, combining
the spectacular with the peaceful.

The remaining counties of Armagh, Cavan, Fermanagh, Monaghan
and Tyrone are all land-locked, but each has its own individual charm,
with water never too far away. Fermanagh, often referred to as
'Ireland's lake district', is dominated by both Upper and Lower Lough
Erne, while Armagh and Tyrone are two of five Ulster counties to
share the shores of Lough Neagh, Ireland's largest freshwater lake.

County Antrim

Contae Aontroma

County Antrim is bounded to the north-east by the narrow Northern Channel of the Irish Sea, and at its closest point, is separated from Scotland by just over ten miles. Its boundary to the south includes the city of Belfast, and this accounts for it being the second most densely-populated county on the island next to Dublin.

As with many other parts of Ireland, County Antrim is endowed with evocative names, and is rich in history, folklore and legends of giants and kings. It easily deserves its reputation as one of the island's most beautiful counties, with widely varying landscapes ranging from chalky coastal cliffs to the unique geological basalt features of the Giant's Causeway, and from enchanted glens to the imposing Slemish Mountain where St Patrick is said to have herded sheep as a young boy. Superb examples of medieval remains can also be found, such as those at Dunluce Castle perched precariously on the north coast, acknowledged as the most impressive ruins in the province.

The well sign-posted 'Causeway Coastal Route' offers the ideal way to begin exploring County Antrim and the province of Ulster. Travelling north from Belfast, Northern Ireland's capital, the road hugs the north coast of Belfast Lough, passing through the town of Carrickfergus with its restored Anglo-Norman Castle, steeped in over 800 years of turbulent history. A few miles further on is the port of Larne, one of the landing points for many of the 'Planters' from Britain during the 17th century. From here the road rises and falls as it winds its way lazily up the coast, offering scenic surprises around almost every headland, and views of Scotland to the east on clear days.

The charming town of Glenarm marks the beginning of the famous Glens of Antrim. The nine glens, formed thousands of years ago when the glaciers of the last Ice Age retreated slowly eastwards towards Scotland, are now clad with moorland, farmland and forest, hiding endless walking trails, rivers, lakes and waterfalls. Many legends have their origins in the Glens, and curses, charms and cures for ailments, leprechauns, banshees and the hawthorn fairy trees are all sources of enchanting stories from days long gone. Old, gnarled hawthorn trees can still be seen in the middle of otherwise clear fields, left there because of the superstition that to cut them down would bring bad fortune to the farmer.

A panoramic view of Belfast Lough and the start of the Antrim coast

The Glens end at the seaside resort of Ballycastle which lies to the south of Rathlin Island. The Island is a popular place for bird watchers and home to Bruce's Cave where Robert the Bruce of Scotland lived in hiding for three months.

Passing spectacular Whitepark Bay, the Giant's Causeway, the town of Bushmills, (home to the world's oldest legal whiskey distillery) and the ruins of Dunluce Castle, the Antrim coast ends at Portrush, a popular seaside resort with its sand-duned golden strand stretching to Ramore Head.

OPPOSITE
Carrickfergus Castle
One of the best preserved Norman castles in Ireland

OVERLEAF: **Glenariff**
Antrim is justly proud of the beauty and serenity of its nine glens, each with its own myths and legends.

LEFT: **Glenoe village**

Cushendun
The original square in the village of Cushendun was designed by Sir Bertram Clough Williams-Ellis, knighted in 1971 for his 'services to architecture and the environment'.

OPPOSITE: Slemish Mountain where, legend tells us,
St Patrick spent six years as a shepherd boy.

Slemish is one of the clearest pieces of evidence of the area's volcanic
past. It is a huge plug in the earth where magma oozed to the surface.

RIGHT: Glenoe waterfall

BELOW: Autumn leaves in Glenariff

Glenariff Forest Park

The Tree Tunnel,
near the village of Stranocum

Bluebells in Glenariff

Ballintoy

A mixture of dark basalt and white limestone rocks merge to a uniform silhouette at dusk.

OPPOSITE

The Carrick-a-Rede rope bridge

Originally, this was a seasonal working bridge for fishermen, but since the demise of salmon fishing along the coast, the rope bridge has become a tourist attraction.
Not for the faint-hearted, the single-file bridge is strung 100 feet (nearly 30 metres) above the waters below.

RIGHT

The White Rocks and Great Arch, east of Portrush

Ireland has a remarkable variety of bedrock and the Antrim coastline exposes just some of it. These are limestone cliffs, but within just a few miles, basalt, shale and sandstone can also be found.

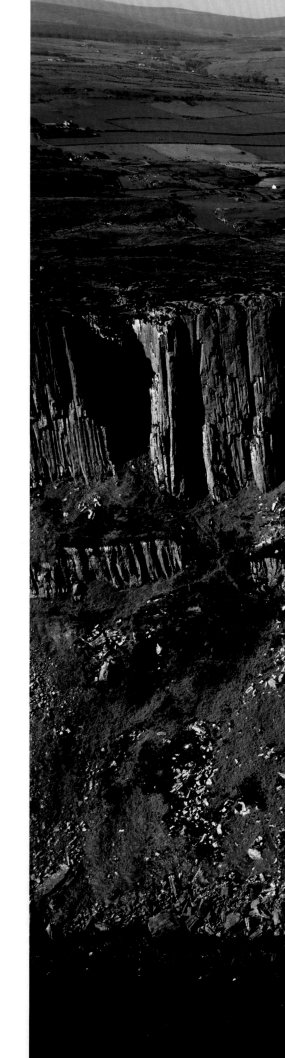

Fair Head on the Antrim coast from Rathlin Island

Rathlin Island was the first landing point of the Vikings in Ireland where they burnt a church in AD 795. This would have been their first view of our mainland, a country they would continue to raid for the next two centuries.

Fair Head

This aerial view of the three-mile (nearly five kilometres) stretch of Fair Head shows why it is so popular with rock climbers. At over 300 feet (nearly 100 metres) high for much of its length, they claim that it is the greatest expanse of climbable rock in Britain and Ireland.

ABOVE

Kinbane Castle

A steep twisting path has to be negotiated to get down to what little there is left of this 16th century castle. Its former glory can only be imagined, positioned in a secluded bay, looking out towards Fair Head and Rathlin Island on the horizon.

RIGHT

The mouth of the River Bush

In the early 17th century, water mills erected by the river formed the beginnings of a town that would later become famous for its whiskey. Bushmills was granted a 'license to distil' by King James 1 in 1608, giving it claim to being the oldest licensed distillery in the world.

OPPOSITE

Dunluce Castle

Perched on the north coast with terrifyingly steep drops on either side, Dunluce is the most extensive ruin of a medieval castle in the province.

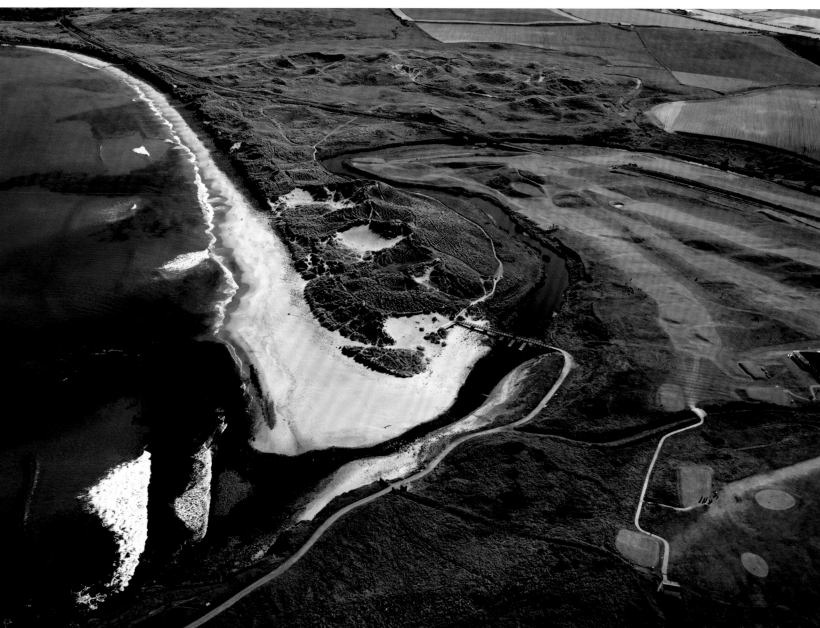

RIGHT AND BELOW

Dunluce Castle

The limestone cliffs of the White Rocks end abruptly against a dark basalt outcrop between the towns of Portballintrae and Portrush. One would think this to be the perfect location for a medieval castle and indeed it was for over 400 years, but its use came to an abrupt end in 1639 when part of the kitchen collapsed into the sea, killing all the kitchen staff in the process.

FAR LEFT
The Glendun River making its way towards the village of Cushendun where its journey ends.

LEFT
Croaghan mountain

The Giant's Causeway

It was 1693 before the Giant's Causeway was brought to the attention of the outside world and first recorded in print by the Royal Geographical Society. It quickly became the subject of a great deal of controversy concerning the origins of volcanic rocks, and is now known internationally for its contribution to the growth of geology as a science. But this natural phenomenon is not just for our earth scientists to ponder. Many simply enjoy the scenic value of 'the stones' and, regardless of the time of day or quality of light, they never fail to fascinate. The Causeway became Northern Ireland's first UNESCO World Heritage Site when it was inscribed in 1986, and today attracts up to 500,000 visitors a year.

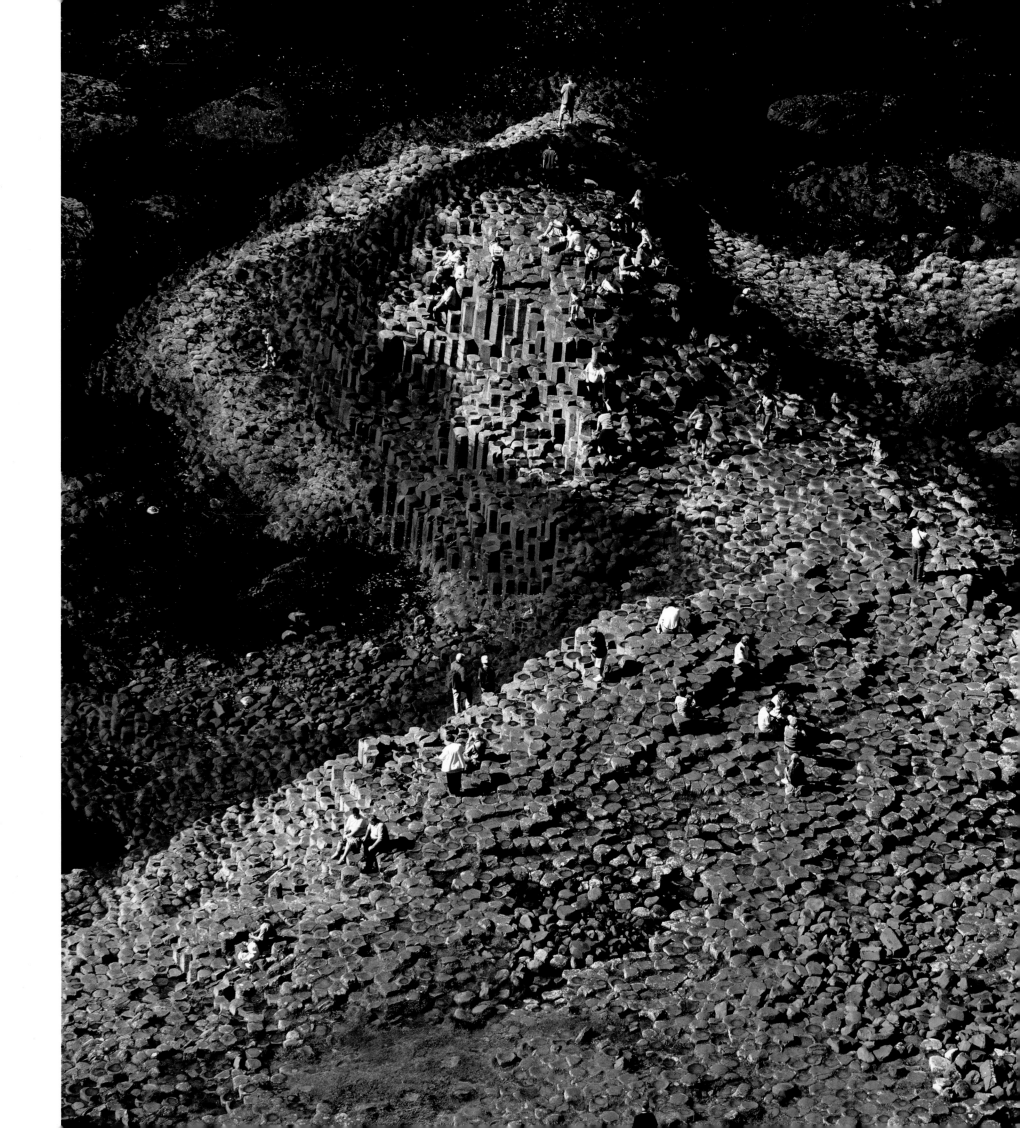

There are many legends associated with the Giant's Causeway, but all agree that it was the warrior and chief of the King of Ireland's armies, Irish giant Finn McCool, who built the causeway so that he could walk to Scotland to fight his Scottish counterpart, Benandonner. Interestingly, the legend corresponds with geological evidence, for there are similar basalt formations, part of the same ancient lava flow, at the site of Fingal's Cave on the Isle of Staffa off the west coast of Scotland.

The harbour at Portrush

The East Strand at Portrush
Limestone stacks and boulders mark the
start of the strand that sweeps round to
the popular seaside resort of Portrush.

County Londonderry
Contae Doire

Looking east across the bay to the seaside town of Portstewart at dusk

The former county of Coleraine and the city of Derry had their names changed to Londonderry in 1613 at the behest of the London Livery Companies who controlled trade and construction throughout the country at the time. To this day, both the county and the city names are subject to the Derry/Londonderry dispute, with the form Derry being preferred by Nationalists and Londonderry by Unionists. Irish humour takes many forms, and one radio presenter from the city strikes a chord with both sides of the community in his solution to the problem. The oblique between the words Derry/Londonderry is locally called a 'stroke', and when the city needs a mention he refers to it as Stroke City.

The county's coast line, from just west of Portrush, passes another pleasant seaside town at Portstewart, its three-mile strand ending at the mouth of the river Bann. Much of the river's course marks the border between the counties of Londonderry and Antrim. Beyond the Bann's mouth, Ireland's longest beach, Magilligan Strand, stretches for six miles to Magilligan Point at the end of Lough Foyle. At the mouth of the river Foyle the county's border wraps round the entire city of Derry, as it creeps into the Inishowen Peninsula.

From early peaceful beginnings, the city of Derry has a long and tumultuous history. *Doire* in Irish means 'Oak Grove' and refers to the original oak grove where St Columb founded his first monastery in the 6th century.

The spire of the present day St Columb's Cathedral dominates the skyline from all approaches to the city and is one of the most important 17th-century buildings in the country. Built in 1633, it was the first specifically Protestant cathedral erected in these islands following the Reformation.

Among the many other historic monuments in Derry, the massive city walls on the west bank of the Foyle are the most striking and memorable. At the time of the 'Plantation of Ulster', businessmen from London sent master-builders to erect the walls and reconstruct what had become a ruined medieval town by that time. It was their duty, under a

Royal Charter of King James I, 'to build and maintain the Derry Walls to help control the local Irish rebels'. In return, they were given large parcels of land in the region. Despite sieges in 1641, 1649 and the Great Siege of 1689, Derry's Walls were never breached – a testimony to their careful planning and excellent construction, and the reason why Derry now bears the title, 'The Maiden City'.

The Great Siege, when Catholic King James II lay siege to the walled city that harboured the local Protestant population, is another part of Ulster's history which brings to the fore the tensions between Catholics and Protestants that existed across the province as a whole. Thirteen (Protestant) Apprentice Boys shut the gates against the oncoming (Catholic) army, and when King James demanded their surrender, it resulted in the now famous Ulster Protestant retort of 'No Surrender'. It was a sad reflection of this event that in 1969, nearly 300 years later, the annual celebratory Apprentice Boys parade along the walls of Derry sparked off protest from the nearby Nationalist Bogside area of the city. It resulted in a riot lasting three days and the British Army was called in to restore order. Widespread violence erupted elsewhere in Northern Ireland as a result, and it is commonly seen as one of the first major confrontations in the conflict that became known as 'the Troubles'.

Just outside the city walls sits the fine, late 19th-century sandstone Guildhall, its stained-glass windows illustrating almost every episode of note in the city's history.

The county also boasts evidence of the earliest known human settlement in Ireland. The discovery was made in the 1970s when, on a site at Mountsandel, south of the university town of Coleraine, a team of archaeologists unearthed a Mesolithic settlement dating back to 7600 BC.

RIGHT: Waterfall at Downhill

FAR RIGHT: River Roe in Roe Valley Country Park

BELOW

The Mussenden Temple from Downhill Strand

Modelled on the Temple of Vesta in Tivoli, the circular sandstone building was built in 1785 by Frederick Hervey, Bishop of Derry, as a library for the once elegant 18th-century mansion at Downhill Demesne.

Looking west along Portstewart strand in early morning light

RIGHT
The Bishop's Gate

One of two gates that lead into the Downhill Demesne.

FAR RIGHT
The Guildhall in Derry

Built in the late 19th century, the sandstone Guildhall was named in honour of the London guilds that supplied the funding, and was officially opened in 1890 as the administrative centre of the Londonderry Corporation. Today, the council chamber on the ground floor is the seat of Derry City Council.

BELOW
Binevenagh Lake

Springhill
A 17th-century 'Planters'
house near Moneymore

Dungiven Castle
Originally the castle was
the ancestral home of the
O'Cahan clan who ruled the
area between the 12th and
17th centuries.

Greencastle

County Donegal

Contae Dhún na nGall

Bog cotton at Rossgull
near Horn Head

During 'the Troubles' (late 1960s to late 1990s), the border between Northern Ireland and the Republic of Ireland was indicated on many roads by heavily-guarded and intimidating Army check points. Since the long-awaited agreement of May 2007 – a commitment between Unionists and Nationalists to share power and restore the Northern Ireland Executive – these have been removed, and nowadays, the only way the traveller knows they have crossed the border is by the 'Welcome' notices and the change of appearance in road signs (Northern Ireland's have black and red symbols on a white background with distance measured in miles whereas the Republic's are black on a yellow background with distance indicated in kilometres). With the province of Ulster comprising six counties in one country and three in the other, our tour encounters this confusing situation on four different occasions as we cross the border from Northern Ireland to 'the South' and back again.

Being one of the province's three counties allied to the Republic of Ireland, it seems ironic that only six miles of Donegal actually borders the rest of the Republic (where it meets County Leitrim). The entire inland east side of the county rubs shoulders with the Northern Ireland counties of Fermanagh, Tyrone and Derry, while the remaining two hundred miles of spectacular Atlantic coast complete the boundary.

Passing through Derry and over the border into the Republic we come to the Inishowen Peninsula, an area with such a range of sights and attractions that it has often been referred to as 'Ireland in Miniature'. The main road here from Derry points westward towards the county's principal town of Letterkenny, but it would be a shame to miss the opportunity to drive around the peninsula which boasts Ireland's most northerly point, Malin Head.

Regardless of what may be found on Inishowen, there are many who would say that the entire county of Donegal possesses the finest scenery in the whole of Ireland. The often jagged coastline is composed of an intoxicating mix of headlands, promontories and peninsulas, with miles of golden beaches rising from sea level to almost 2000 feet (606 metres) at Slieve League, the second highest coastal cliffs in Europe next to those at Croaghaun on Achill Island in County Mayo.

Between coast and inland border, the landscape varies extensively. Stripped of much of its soil by the Ice Age, it is generally a poor agricultural area, and it is characteristic of the Donegal landscape that the undulating roads across almost endless heather and grass-covered bogland can be traversed for miles at a time without any sign of human habitation. From the starkness of sheep-strewn moorland and turf-cut bogs, the county also boasts two major mountain ranges, the Derryveagh Mountains in the north and the Bluestack Mountains in the south. Between them, they harbour hundreds of small to large-sized peaks with the unmistakable quartzite, conically-shaped Errigal Mountain in the Derryveagh range crowning them all at nearly 2500 feet (751 metres).

Donegal also has more than its share of ancient history sites – dolmens, court cairns and stone circles – but its two stone forts at Grianán of Aileach and Doon are outstanding. Not far from the border and with commanding views over Lough Foyle, Lough Swilly and the city of Derry, Grianán of Aileach sits on the top of Greenan Mountain, and is acknowledged as one of the finest stone forts in Ireland. Near the pretty town of Portnoo in the south-west of the county, Doon Fort is a rare example of a stone fort on a crannog, a man-made island built purely for extra protection.

LEFT: Looking south west towards Tullagh Bay from Malin Head

Malin Head on the Inishowen peninsula in Donegal is the most northerly point of Ireland.

ABOVE: Knockalla Beach

One of the most beautiful beaches in Ireland stretches two miles across Ballymastocker Bay, near the village of Portsalon on the Fanad peninsula.

Snow capped Mount Errigal

The Poisoned Glen below Mount Errigal

There are many stories which account for the incongruous name of this beautiful glen, with tales of a poisoned river and plants, and of a place where birds don't nest. However, the explanation considered to be most likely is much more ordinary. The original Irish name translates as the 'Heavenly Glen', but it is thought that an English cartographer confused the Irish words for 'heaven' (*neamh*) and 'poison' (*nimh*) which are quite similar in spelling, if not pronunciation, so giving the name commonly used today.

Sand dunes at Ballyness Bay, with the Derryveagh Mountains beyond

Doon Fort
A rare example of a stone fort on a crannog, a man-made island built for extra protection

Slieve League, the second highest sea cliffs in Europe

Grianán of Aileach

Grianán means 'sun temple' in Irish and is derived from 'Grainne, the Sun Goddess'. Whilst the bank and ditch date back to the Iron Age, the walls were probably built in the early Christian era. It was reconstructed in 1870 and is regarded as one of the finest examples of a stone fort in Ireland.

LEFT

Kilclooney More Dolmen

Near the town of Ardara in west Donegal the portals of this dolmen are six feet (nearly two metres) tall and the massive 20 feet (over six metres) capstone is angled as if poised for flight.

BELOW

Trannarossa Bay near Downings

Standing stone at Glencolumbkille

Glencolumbkille, 'The Glen of St Colmcille', is named after one of Ireland's most famous missionary monks, more often referred to as Columba of Iona.

Glencolumbkille valley and village are scattered with crosses and stone carved monolithic memories of its much-loved patron who lived here with followers in the 6th century. Every year, on the 9th of June, he is still remembered when pilgrims undertake a three mile procession in bare feet.

Here, two symbols of worship can be seen, separated in time by thousands of years.

LEFT

Glengesh, near Ardara

A corkscrew road winds its way through this carved out pass to Glencolumbkille.

Looking back from Horn Head towards Dunfanaghy

Hidden treasures are to be discovered throughout Donegal whenever a turn off the main road is taken, especially towards the coast. A minor road from the town of Dunfanaghy on to the small northern promontory of Horn Head provided this view, with the Derryveagh Mountains in the background.

BELOW

The Murder Hole, Rosguill

At the far end of Rosguill, yet another small headland on this sculptured coastline has both beauty and tragedy attached. The description of a 'hole' is a contradiction to the ridged beach, exposed at low tide when the sea drops on either side. The tale of murder is linked to the story of a local man whose wife mysteriously disappeared, thought by many to have been thrown by him from the cliffs into the raging sea below.

The deserted village of Port,
near Glencolumbkille

County Tyrone

Contae Thír Eoghain

Crossing the boundary lines between Ireland's counties never presents a *sudden* change of scenery, but some counties certainly have their individual characteristics. Leaving Donegal's varied tapestry of landscapes and crossing back again into Northern Ireland, Tyrone's pleasant rolling hills can make certain routes appear very uniform, although the skyline to the north is broken by the Sperrin Mountains which it shares with neighbouring County Derry. The Sperrins' southern slopes, threaded by streams and small roads, gently spill their contoured range over the picturesque Glenelly Valley towards Tyrone's county town of Omagh, and a drive along the road that hugs the Glenelly river really is worthwhile. Another treat is to be found at Gortin Glen Forest Park, six miles north of Omagh, where the five-mile recreational drive offers some breathtaking views.

Apart from the main towns of Omagh, Cookstown and Dungannon, the unscarred bogland landscape, while almost devoid of inhabitants, is rich in prehistoric and Celtic remains, with over 1000 standing stones bearing testament to the Stone Age people who passed this way. The Beaghmore Stone Circles were discovered by accident during turf cutting in the 1940s, and four years of excavation to remove a thick layer of protective turf eventually uncovered nearly 1,300 stones.

Historically, Tyrone was the traditional stronghold of the ruling O'Neill clans, the greatest of the Gaelic Irish families in Ulster. They survived into the 17th century when Hugh O'Neill, chief of Tyrone, lost the landmark battle against the English. Thus began a dark time in Ulster's history, the demise of the O'Neill clan bringing down the curtain on a political and cultural era after which the province could no longer compete with its British neighbour, while the 'Plantation of Ulster' which followed was to change it forever.

Ireland's constantly changing skies can bring dramatic effects to even the most gentle of scenes.

Errigal Keerogue Cross, near Augher

The ancient ecclesiastical site provides a splendid view over the Clogher valley.

Gortin River

OPPOSITE
Gortin Lake

RIGHT
Grazing in the Sperrin Mountains

FAR RIGHT
Church near Dunamanagh, Plumbridge, Gortin Valley

BELOW
Gortin Valley

Beaghmore Stone Circles

Beaghmore, 'moor of the birches', was first
discovered in the mid to late 1940s under a thick
layer of peat, a dominating feature of this area.
The circles and rows are thought to date from
between 2000 and 1200 BC (the early Bronze Age).
Their exact purpose remains unknown, although in
some cases, their alignment correlates with the
movement of the sun, moon and stars. Twelve
round cairns (burial mounds) were also found in
the area, legacies of our ancient forefathers'
beliefs and fears.

OPPOSITE
Dusk over Lough Beg

RIGHT
Mourne River

BELOW
Gortin Valley

Devenish Island

On the south end of Lower Lough Erne, Devenish Island is a truly holy place. Across its centre lie a series of ruined medieval buildings and a well-preserved round tower, interspersed with headstones and crosses.

The site dates back to the 6th century when the earliest monastery was founded by St Molaise. With the ruins bathed in serene evening light, it becomes easy to imagine what it must have been like in its heyday, when upwards of 1500 monks and scholars lived and worked here.

Sunset over Lower Lough Erne looking towards Devenish

Leaving behind the rolling hills of County Tyrone yet remaining in Northern Ireland, the water-strewn county of Fermanagh presents another contrast on our provincial journey. Ulster's majestic river Erne has its source in County Cavan and eventually enters the Atlantic Ocean at Ballyshannon in County Donegal. Between the two counties, its winding journey brings it through Fermanagh where it has formed one of the most impressive lakes in the whole of Europe. Made up of two channels, the reed-fringed Lower and Upper Loughs dominate the county and have earned it the title of 'Ireland's lake district'.

Lough Erne is a veritable paradise for lovers of water sports, and as an integral part of the Shannon-Erne Waterway, cruisers are frequently to be seen during the summer months. With fishing, water-skiing and canoeing proving to be popular pastimes too, it would be easy to conclude that Fermanagh is just about water-based activities. But while this is true to a large extent, there is also much more of general and historic interest in the region.

Covering nearly a third of the county, the surface of the lake is dotted with islands, many holding secrets of pre-Christian spiritual worship and of later medieval monastic life. There is evidence of extensive Stone Age activity throughout Fermanagh (stone circles, court cairns and passage cairns), with much more believed to be still lying beneath the blanket bogs in the north of the county.

The local debate about whether Lough Erne is in Fermanagh or Fermanagh in Lough Erne gives the impression that the entire county is not only wet but flat. Not so, for the Cuilagh Mountains, shared with neighbouring Cavan, lie in the south-west of the county. Deep beneath their peaks can be found the natural wonder of the Marble Arch Caves, a fine example of a hidden underworld of rivers, glistening stalactites, waterfalls, winding passages and bewildering cave formations. The Caves have been designated as one of 31 European Geoparks.

The county town of Enniskillen is situated largely on an island in the river between the Upper and Lower Loughs, where the 15th-century Enniskillen Castle still stands guard. Across the bridge from the Castle is Portora Royal School whose former pupils include two of Ireland's famous literary figures, Oscar Wilde and Samuel Beckett.

Other buildings of note in the county date from the 18th century, when some of Fermanagh's most successful 'Planters' built impressive mansions such as Colebrooke House, Florence Court and Castle Coole, the latter two now under the control and care of the National Trust.

Enniskillen Castle

First built in the 15th century, Enniskillen Castle has witnessed many battles and sieges throughout its turbulent life. An English garrison fort in the 17th century, it was eventually remodelled as a military barracks in the 18th. Today, beautifully restored, it is home to two museums.

The 17th-century Plantation of Ulster not only brought about improvement in many of Ulster's existing towns but also prompted the establishment of many new towns, the construction of factories to accommodate new industries and the building of grand houses for the new 'landed gentry'.

LEFT: Castle Coole

Wealthy heir Armar Lowry-Corry, 1st Earl of Belmore, was the Earl of Enniskillen's brother-in-law, and although he originally built Castle Coole as a summer retreat, he always intended it to outshine Florence Court. Portland stone was specially shipped from England to build it and the final cost was £57,000, equivalent to approximately £25million today.

ABOVE: Colebrooke Park House, Brookeborough

The name of Colebrooke derives from the marriage of Major Thomas Brooke to Catherine Cole in the 17th century. To this day the house and 1,000 acre estate have been in the hands of the Brookes, presently the family home of Lord and Lady Brookeborough.

LEFT: Belle Isle Castle, near Lisbellaw

With origins going back to the end of the 17th century, the Belle Isle Estate is presently owned by the Duke of Abercorn who has extensively and sensitively refurbished the castle, nearby courtyard and cottages as holiday accommodation.

OPPOSITE: Florence Court

Sir John Cole of Enniskillen first built a house on the site in the early 18th century for his Cornish wife Florence, naming it after her. Subsequent members of the Cole family, having been granted the title, Earl of Enniskillen, built the three-storey greystone Georgian mansion which now occupies the site, its name retaining the original tribute to Florence.

Lower Lough Erne

FAR LEFT: The Janus Stone in Caldragh Cemetery, Boa Island

Boa in Irish is *badhbha*, meaning 'war goddess', yet this ancient Celtic figure is obviously male. It stands about three feet (one metre) high among old grave stones and actually has two faces and bodies, back to back. Many conjectures have been made about its function in Celtic society – a spirit to invoke fertility perhaps, or a war god – but whatever the truth, it certainly seems to have been a powerful deity of its time.

LEFT: Monea Castle

One of the best preserved Planter's castles built in 1618. It was destroyed by fire in the Great Rebellion of 1641.

BELOW: Lower Lough Erne

County Cavan

Contae an Cabhán

Crossing back into the Republic of Ireland to County Cavan, there are again many reminders of the country's 6,000-year heritage, the west of the county in particular featuring an abundance of Stone Age archaeological sites. However, they can be difficult to find for Cavan is a county where it is easy to lose your bearings. Criss-crossed by an intricate pattern of roads and lanes built to dodge the small hills and lakes, the topography is far from varied and can be confusing for visitors.

In the early 17th century and following a similar pattern to other counties in Ulster, 'Planters' from England and Scotland laid the foundations for many of Cavan's towns and villages, including Virginia, named for Elizabeth I, the 'Virgin Queen'. It was they who helped the county prosper, primarily through the growth of the linen and wool industries. In Irish, the word *cavan* means 'a hollow', and indeed, the county lies in the lowlands of the country. Similarly, its main town,

which takes the county name, lies in its own smaller hollow among the hills.

Until the early 1990s, County Cavan tended to be overlooked by tourists and holiday makers. While it may not possess the dramatic landscapes of some of its neighbouring counties, this land-locked region with its meandering rivers, streams and tree-lined lakes provides excellent opportunities for those visitors interested in fishing.

The county is famous for being the source of two great Irish rivers. The Shannon, the longest river in Ireland, has its source at the mystical Shannon Pot, just north of the village of Dowra, while the River Erne has its origins at Lough Gowna before it journeys northwest. Both rivers combine to form one of the great water channels in Europe, the Shannon–Erne Waterway, which links the Republic with Northern Ireland and takes in all four provinces in the process. The major redevelopment of the Ballinamore–Ballyconnell Canal on the Waterway, completed in 1994, now makes it possible to travel by boat through the entire county and consequently has made a significant difference to Cavan's popularity with tourists.

Locals will tell you that Cavan has 365 lakes – one for each day of the year (by coincidence you may also hear the same claim about Strangford Lough in County Down and Clew Bay in County Mayo). Exaggeration it may be, but the point comes across, for wherever you are in the county, water is never far away. Situated in the drumlin belt of the north of Ireland's Central Plain, Cavan has no high ground to speak of, and what low hills it has are interlaced with the gentle watery landscape that is typical of the area. A perfect example is the complex confusion of lakes that makes up Lough Oughter, internationally renowned for its coarse angling, and home to the imposing Cloughoughter Castle.

Cromwell's Bridge in Dún an Rí Forest Park

Named because Oliver Cromwell crossed this bridge on his way to attack a neighbouring castle

**Cloughoughter Castle on
Lough Oughter at sunrise**

Originally built in the early 13th century,
Cloughoughter Castle was the last
stronghold to fall in the Cromwellian wars.
Immediately afterwards, in March 1653, it
was destroyed and rendered useless by a
massive explosion of gunpowder.

LEFT: Overlooking the town of Virginia

Sunset over Lough Oughter

Reed fringed Lough Ramor

LEFT: River Erne at Belturbet

In Ireland's earlier battling days the town of Belturbet, hidden here behind
the trees, was originally built as a strategic point of defence against invaders.
Today its invaders are anglers and boating enthusiasts.

County Monaghan
Contae an Mhuineacháin

While Cavan is mostly associated with lakes, neighbouring County Monaghan is best known as drumlin country.

Described in textbooks as 'basket of eggs' topography, drumlins are softly-rounded mounds of land which were formed by retreating glaciers at the end of the last Ice Age. Now covered by soil and grass, hedgerows stretch across them marking out the fields where cattle graze and crops are grown. The gentle curves of the land are quite charming but unrelentingly repetitive, for once you are over one small hill the next seems much the same. Occasionally a lake comes into view offering a respite from the endlessly undulating landscape, but they are far less numerous than in neighbouring County Cavan. The curiously-shaped hillocks also dictate the pattern of the country roads that meander round them, with the north of the county in particular scored by a web of interlaced lanes and roadways.

Patrick Kavanagh, one of Ireland's most renowned poets of the 20th century, was born in Inniskeen in the south of the county, and in many of his poems, such as 'Having to Live in the Country', he both celebrates and criticises the county's hedged-in landscape.

Influences of the 17th-century 'Planters' are clearly to be seen in the Gothic and Presbyterian churches and architecture of the county's well-planned towns (especially in Monaghan itself), and in other impressive buildings, such as Hilton Park, Hope Castle and Castle Leslie.

Castle Leslie is a secluded private estate covering 1,000 acres (405 hectares) of rolling countryside dotted with ancient woodland and glittering lakes. One of only thirty great Irish castle estates still run by the original family, the Leslies have lived here since the 1660s, welcoming visits by everyone from politicians to poets.

LEFT: Typical drumlin country

Round Tower at Clones

RIGHT: Castle Leslie, Glaslough

Now the site of a luxurious country club, the 1,000-acre Castle Leslie estate in County Monaghan first came into the hands of the Leslie family in the 17th century. Bishop John Leslie bought Glaslough Castle and estate in 1665 with £2,000 he received as a reward for defending Charles II against Cromwell at the Battle of Raphoe. The main feature of the present-day estate is a Scottish baronial-style Castle, constructed on the site of the old one in the 1870s and designed by Sir Charles Lanyon and W.H. Lynn for the 1st Baronet, Sir John Leslie MP. It is home to the family's many beautiful antiques and heirlooms, including Winston Churchill's christening robe (the Leslies are related to the Churchill family). The Estate also boasts several lakes, large forests and a Hunting Lodge. It is perhaps best known today as the location for the wedding of Sir Paul McCartney and Heather Mills in 2002.

ABOVE: Hope Castle, near Castleblaney

Hope Castle was built in the 18th century on the site of the former Blayney Castle, from which the town derived its name. It has had many owners and uses over the years – at one point it was a convent, and later became the home of Queen Victoria's son, Prince Arthur the Duke of Connacht and his family.

RIGHT: Hilton Park, near Clones

This fine 18th-century house has been in the Madden family since 1734. The estate features two lakes and extensive woodland, with many species of trees and shrubs collected from foreign lands by travelling Maddens over the centuries.

OPPOSITE: Lough Muckno

ABOVE: High Cross at Clones

ABOVE RIGHT: One of two lakes at Hilton Park

FAR RIGHT: Pathway walk at Castle Leslie

RIGHT: River Dromore

County Armagh

Contae Ard Macha

Apple blossom in the 'Orchard County'

The romantic and haunting ballad of 'The Boys from County Armagh' can often be heard sung with pride by many Armaghians, especially when they are 'far across the foam'. But its lyrics make no mention of the trouble and strife – both recent and ancient – which the county has endured.

Traditionally known as the Orchard County because much of it has been given over to apple growing, Armagh has also earned itself a less attractive reputation. With the partition of Ireland in 1922 which split the province of Ulster between Northern Ireland and the Republic, nearly half of Armagh's boundary forms the border between the two countries (where it joins Monaghan and Louth), and during 'the Troubles' (late 1960s to the late 1990s), the southern part of the county became the most militarised region in Western Europe. It was a heartland of Republican activity during that time, and as a result, was irreverently nicknamed 'Bandit Country' by many in Northern Ireland, including some of Armagh's own residents.

With 'the Troubles' now a thing of the past and the reminders of military occupation removed, the county's picturesque landscape has been restored to its former glory, and tourists, long deterred from visiting the county, can now rediscover its many charms. It is a delightful part of the province – a land of great contrast and diversity. Few areas of similar extent can show such a variety of landforms and topography, with its bold contrast of mountains and lowlands. Most of its lakes are concentrated in and around the area known as the Ring of Gullion, a naturally formed ring-dyke of low-lying hills encircling Slieve Gullion, one of the most mysteriously beautiful mountains in the country.

The county's capital is Armagh, although its northerly neighbours, Lurgan and Portadown, have larger populations. For long the county town, Armagh was finally granted City status in the mid-1990s, a rank more appropriate to its unique significance in the religious history of Ireland. In his mission to convert Ireland to Christianity, Saint Patrick chose Armagh as the centre for the new religion. In AD 445 he established his church on what is now known as Cathedral Close, declaring that it should take precedence over all other churches in Ireland. Saint Patrick also decreed that only those educated in Armagh could spread the gospel. Since then, it has been regarded as the ecclesiastical capital of the entire country and an important educational centre, giving rise to its claim to be the city of Saints and Scholars.

Today, there are two St Patrick's Cathedrals in the city – one Protestant and one Roman Catholic – with both, under the leadership of their respective Archbishops, working closely together in the spirit of Ireland's patron saint. However, there are those who would claim that the two Cathedrals, which sit on different hills in the city, are more like 'the horns of a dilemma', symbolising the lack of interaction between the two communities.

Legend dictates that Brian Boru, High King of Ireland, was buried on the 'north side of the great church' where the Protestant Cathedral now stands. Boru died in battle after he brought together many of the Irish Kings and Chieftains to defeat the Vikings in Ireland at the Battle of Clontarf in 1014.

A few miles west of the city are the remains of Navan Fort, the former ancient seat of northern power for nearly 700 years (it rivalled Tara in the south). It was here that the Kings of Ulster ruled, where Queen Macha built her palace and where the Knights of the Red Branch were based alongside their greatest champion, Cúchulainn.

ABOVE: Tassagh Railway Viaduct, near Keady

Constructed across the Tassagh valley between
1903 and 1910 by the Castleblayney, Keady and
Armagh Railway

RIGHT: From Slieve Gullion

A naturally formed ring-dyke of low-lying hills
encircles Slieve Gullion, one of the most
mysteriously beautiful scenes in the country. In
Irish *sliabh gCuilinn* means 'the mountain of
Culainn', and many legends are attached to it,
the best known relating to Cúchulainn, the
famous 'Hound of Ulster', who took his name
here after slaying the hound (*Cú*) of the
blacksmith Culainn.

RIGHT: **Kilnasaggart Pillar Stone**

The slim granite pillar stone is seven feet (just over two metres) high and is inscribed with no less than 13 crosses. There is also a written inscription dating the stone to c. AD 700, making it one of the earliest Christian monuments in Ireland.

FAR RIGHT: **Tynan Cross**

Dating from AD 800–900, the cross is almost all that is left of the original monastery founded in the village of Tynan in the west of the county.

BELOW: **Ballykeel Tomb**

The seven feet (2.1 metres) high portals support a 12 feet (3.65 metres) capstone. It was excavated in 1963, with a variety of early Neolithic pottery being discovered.

BELOW RIGHT: **Clontygora Cairn**

Excavated in 1937, local people refer to the cairn as 'the King's Ring'. It has an unusually deep court that nearly forms a full circle.

OPPOSITE: **Moyry Castle**

The castle was built near the border between Ulster and Leinster in 1601 by Lord Mountjoy, Lord Deputy and Lord Lieutenant of Ireland, to secure the vital Moyry Pass, then described as the 'gap of the north'.

Armagh's cathedrals are sited on two of the seven hills on which the city is built.

A statue of Saint Patrick, Ireland's patron saint, looks down over Armagh city from the grounds of the Catholic Cathedral.

The Armagh Observatory
Founded in 1789, the observatory is the oldest meteorological station in Ireland.

LEFT: St Patrick's Catholic Cathedral

FAR LEFT: St Patrick's Protestant Cathedral

Navan Fort

Much of Armagh's ancient history is centred on the establishment of the
legendary Navan Fort or 'Emain Macha', founded by the pagan Queen Macha.
Although people occupied the site from the Stone Age to the Middle Ages,
most of the construction took place between 400 and 100 BC.

All that remains today is a ditched enclosure around a curved mound, about
1000 feet (305 metres) across. Excavation work has found evidence that it had
been a residential site, but was later used for ceremonial purposes. It became
the prehistoric capital of Ulster where the legendary warriors of the Red Branch
of Ulster were based.

County Down
Contae an Dúin

Newforge House, Magheralin
The finely preserved Georgian country house dates from 1785.

Rhododendron petals in Rowallane Gardens, near Saintfield

OVERLEAF
The Mourne Mountains

Ireland's climate is temperate, which usually means warm damp summers and mild wet winters. Here, a rarely seen layer of snow adorns the mountains with the seaside town of Newcastle stretched at their feet.

Another county possessing both beauty and diversity in its neat and compact landscape is the county of Down. Bounded to the north by County Antrim and to the west by County Armagh, our tour is completed by a varied coastline which stretches from Carlingford Lough to Belfast Lough, the former nestling quietly between Down's Mourne Mountains and the Carlingford Mountains in neighbouring County Louth.

Percy French's famous ballad has made it widely-known that 'the Mountains of Mourne sweep down to the sea', and they do so at the seaside town of Newcastle in Dundrum Bay. Amongst the Mourne range are twelve peaks of pink-gray granite over 2000 feet (610 metres) in height, all within an area of 120 square miles (310 square kilometres), and although much of the area is accessible by car, the mountains are ideal for walking, climbing and fell-running. In addition to a number of hidden lakes, the mountains are also home to two large reservoirs, Silent Valley and Ben Crom, which together supply 30 million gallons (136 million litres) of water a day to Belfast and County Down.

A few miles north-east of Newcastle is the town of Downpatrick and the south end of Strangford Lough. Both are intrinsically linked through St Patrick, Ireland's patron saint, who is said to have sailed into the Lough as a young man in AD 432. He died at Downpatrick in 493, and his grave can be found at Down Cathedral in the town.

Strangford Lough could be described as a place where the sea invades the land. Its southern entrance is a deep channel just 550 yards (0.5 kilometre) in width and nearly five miles (eight kilometres) long, forming a narrow gap through which 400 million tons of water rush twice a day into the lough's intertidal zone. The Vikings aptly named it

Strangrfjörthr, meaning 'violent fjord'. Today it is called The Narrows, and the 'violent' waters now pass the town which took its former name – Strangford. On the opposite shore, on the Ards Peninsula, Portaferry is so named because of the car ferry which runs between it and Strangford every 15 minutes.

Like a curled finger pointing down to The Narrows, the Ards Peninsula encloses the Lough, protecting it from the Irish Sea. As a consequence, the two roads that run the length of it on its opposite shores are very different. The sheltered loughside road skirts the shores of the Lough for the most part, offering views of the largest inlet in Ireland where, locals will tell you, there are 365 islands, one for every day of the year. In reality there are only 70, submerged evidence of Ireland's drumlin belt which stretches from County Down to Donegal Bay.

Strangford Lough is an internationally recognised conservation area and an important migration destination for many wading and sea birds, especially the Brent Geese – three-quarters of their entire population winter here.

The breezy coast road on the other side of the peninsula runs north from Portaferry all the way round to Belfast Lough and to Northern Ireland's capital city, passing through the most easterly point of Ireland at the village of Ballyhalbert and the popular seaside resort of Bangor.

Points of interest in the inner county include the birthplace of Patrick Brontë whose three daughters became great novelists. He inspired them by tales of his youth on the banks of the Bann, and its valley, stretching from Banbridge to Rathfriland, is now commonly referred to as 'Brontë Country'.

RIGHT: The Silent Valley Reservoir in the Mournes

Thirty million gallons (136 million litres) of water a day are supplied to Belfast and County Down from the Mournes. The reservoir is well named, for the exhilarating climb will bring you to still waters sheltered on all sides.

Stone walls are a common sight below the Mournes

Widespread glacial deposits have been manually lifted and organised as field dividers, at the same time clearing the land for farming.

Hay stacks near Seaforde, with the Mourne Mountains in the distance

The Mournes, designated one of the province's Areas of Outstanding Natural Beauty and Ulster's highest mountain range, are visited by many tourists, walkers, runners and climbers throughout the year. Some of the mountains have names beginning with Slieve, from the Irish word *sliabh*, meaning 'mountain' – Slieve Donard, Slieve Lamagan and Slieve Muck for example. But there are also a number of other curious names to be found – Pigeon Rock, Buzzard's Roost, the Brandy Pad and the Devil's Coach Road.

Heathers, gorse bushes and bog cotton bring a variation of colour at different times of the year, and these unique landscapes are home to many species of birds. Sadly though, the Golden Eagle, a former inhabitant, has not been seen since the middle of the 19th century.

LEFT: Castlewellan Forest Park
The 19th-century baronial-style castle built by the Annesley family overlooks the lake at Castlewellan Forest Park.

Annalong harbour
One of many small fishing villages to be found on Down's coast.

ABOVE: Parish church of St Malachy, Hillsborough

RIGHT: Cloughmore Stone
The 30-ton granite boulder lying on the Slieve Martin Mountain Ridge is a spectacular remnant from the Ice Age, although local Irish folklore accounts for it in a much more imaginative way. Legend claims that the Irish giant, Finn McCool of Giant's Causeway fame, threw it at an enemy across from the Cooley Mountains on the other side of Carlingford Lough.

Dundrum Castle

The evocative medieval ruins of a castle founded by the legendary Norman adventurer
John de Courcy, following his invasion of Ulster in 1177

Inch Abbey, near Downpatrick

Also founded by John de Courcy but this was in recompense for burning down another
abbey, that of Erenagh, which he believed was fortified against him.

An early morning start on
a farm near Scrabo hill

BELOW LEFT:

Mount Stewart House and Gardens,
near Newtownards

The grand 19th-century house has a splendid interior, but
the magnificent gardens are the main attraction at this
National Trust owned property.

BELOW RIGHT: Ballycopeland Windmill, near Millisle

ABOVE FAR LEFT: St John's Point lighthouse, near Killough

ABOVE CENTRE: Scrabo Tower, near Newtownards

Scrabo is one of County Down's most prominent man-made landmarks. On a clear day, the views from the hill and the summit of the tower are breathtaking across Strangford Lough to the Mourne Mountains in the south, and the Scottish coast to the east.

ABOVE RIGHT: Canadian Brent Geese spend their winters on Strangford Lough

LEFT: Drumlins in Strangford Lough

Belfast
Béal Feirste

Malone House in Barnett Demesne
The peaceful setting of Malone House can be found just ten minutes drive from the city centre, with the Belfast hills in the background and early morning mist rising off the river Lagan below.

Belfast is Northern Ireland's capital city (but not the capital of counties Cavan, Donegal and Monaghan which are in the Republic of Ireland). From the late 1960s to the late 1990s, it had arguably the highest media profile of any city in Europe. Images of sectarian hatred, bombings, murder and political warfare, shown all over the world, rendered Belfast, and to a large extent, the whole of Northern Ireland, a destination that visitors and tourists were often advised to avoid. This perception was an embarrassment for the majority of its residents, and fuelled their determination to eradicate the problem and strive for improvements, both physical and political. Today, those troubled times are a thing of the past, and thanks to the city's resilience, a major process of regeneration is underway.

Ironically, given its recent history and periods of conflict, Belfast began life in relative peace. Without a Celtic or Viking invasion in sight, early settlement seems to have been slow and gradual in a location that is unique. At the southern, inner end of Belfast Lough, the Belfast hills seem to preside over it as they look down from the west over the city which stretches along the valley of the River Lagan.

Following the 'Plantation of Ulster' in the 17th century, Belfast grew steadily from a small village into a robust town. By the 1800s, the development of industries such as linen, rope-making and shipbuilding enabled its population to double in size every ten years, eventually making it the undisputed centre of the industrial revolution in Ireland.

Industrial prosperity had reached its peak by the early 20th century, and following the disruptions of two World Wars it declined considerably. Like many major cities in Ireland and Britain, Belfast had to face the detrimental effects that heavy industry had had on its river. Factories had been depositing their waste in the Lagan for nearly 200 years, and the results were devastating. Slowly but surely, the town planners developed a strategy to counteract this, and while 'the Troubles' were brewing, key city figures hatched the concept of 'Laganside' in order to address the problem. In 1989 the Laganside Corporation, a body involving government, Belfast City Council and the Belfast Harbour Commissioners, was established to promote Laganside as a commercial and tourist opportunity, and to raise the interests of private property developers. Focus was largely on the derelict industrial sites along the river banks, and since Laganside's inception, changes to infrastructure and new building have transformed the city.

An award-winning concert venue (Waterfront Hall), riverside apartments, office blocks and hotels now look down on a dredged, aerated, clean river where fishing, rowing and sailing are commonplace. The Victorian splendour of the city centre now rubs shoulders with modern architecture and sculpture, and Belfast has a vibrancy about it. With lively arts, culture and social scenes, it can confidently describe itself as a European city *par excellence*.

New meets old
The Belfast Eye, the glass dome of the Victoria Centre shopping complex and the 'Thanksgiving' sculpture by internationally acclaimed Andy Scott, sit comfortably alongside the Queen's Bridge and Victorian red brick buildings in Belfast's city centre.

Belfast City Hall

Belfast's 'pride and joy', a symbol of stability for Belfast which has endured such trouble in the past.

There are many examples of grandiose 19th-century architecture to be found in Belfast's public buildings and shopping stores. But the main architectural statement of that era is, without doubt, the City Hall in Donegall Square, the capital's undisputed centre. The building was intended to mark the success and prosperity of the town's industrial achievements, and plans for the building began in 1888, the year Belfast was awarded City status by Queen Victoria. The Portland stone edifice, with its copper – now verdigris green – central dome is a truly fine building, perfectly positioned in the square, surrounded by well-proportioned lawns and adorned with sculptures and statues. Most notable is one of Queen Victoria herself on an imposing plinth in front of the main entrance.

The Crown Liquor Saloon

The Victorian bar has been lovingly restored by its owners, The National Trust, with an interior that features stained-glass, marbling, woodcarving and an ornate plaster ceiling.

ABOVE: **The Palm House, Botanic Gardens**

Built in 1839, this fine example of curvilinear glass and cast iron work was the first hothouse of its kind in the world, and one of many successes for architect Charles Lanyon.

ABOVE LEFT: **Parliament Buildings at Stormont**

The need for a separate parliamentary building for Northern Ireland emerged when the new country was defined in 1920. Part of the interior of Parliament Buildings, known locally as Stormont because of its location, was designed to reflect the House of Commons in London.

Queen's University, Belfast

Brick making, using the clays of the Lagan basin, was also a major industry in the late 18th century, and was responsible for the miles of redbrick terrace houses in the city centre, originally built for the industry's workers. Far from being a cheap building material, the legacy of Belfast's brickworks is also proudly on show in many tree-lined bourgeois avenues further out from the centre, but most splendidly seen in the main building of Queen's University in the south of the city. It was designed by the Sussex-born architect Charles Lanyon who eventually made Ireland his home.

The giant cranes at Harland & Wolff are a familiar landmark on Belfast's skyline, a reminder of the many fine ships and cruise liners built here over the centuries. Most famous was RMS Titanic, thought by many to have been built in Southampton. Belfast was, and still is, very proud, not only of the achievement, but also of the skill and craftsmanship that went along with it. The tragic sinking of the Titanic on its maiden voyage in April 1912 was a terrible blow to all who had worked on it, and there were many reports in the press of the day of men crying in the streets of Belfast. When blame was being attributed to all and sundry, Belfast wits were quick to respond, 'she was in fine working order when she left here'.

Two very different views over Northern Ireland's capital city
RIGHT: from Cavehill, west of the city
BELOW: from the Castlereagh hills in the east

OPPOSITE
An overview of Belfast shows the River Lagan as it winds its way to the Lough.

Redevelopment and regeneration is an ongoing process in Belfast. Based on Queen's Island, the site of the famous Harland and Wolff shipyards, the newly-branded Titanic Quarter has links to the history of the city when it was a world centre of maritime trade, shipbuilding and commerce. Two centuries later, it is playing a leading role in yet another rebirth for the city.

At the gateway to Titanic Quarter stands the Odyssey Complex, a symbol of Belfast's rejuvenation for the new millennium. Attracting over three million visitors in its first year, it has since become home to the city's ice hockey team, the Belfast Giants, and hosted events from concerts to indoor horse jumping. The Odyssey's huge success highlights the massive potential of the Titanic Quarter as a mixed-use waterfront location, thus safeguarding the area's heritage for the future.

RIGHT: The Odyssey Complex, and in the background, Harland and Wolff's iconic yellow cranes, affectionately known locally as Samson and Goliath

BELOW: The rejuvenated River Lagan

Looking over the city to Belfast Lough where RMS Titanic was built and launched in 1912

A haunting view of Dunluce Castle
conjures up images of history, myth
and legend

Published by Booklink and Scenic Ireland, Ireland
Publisher: Dr Claude Costecalde and Christopher Hill

© Photographs, Chris Hill, 2008
© Text, Colin McCadden, 2008
Image processing: Robert Malone, Paul Lindsay
Editor: Dr Averill Buchanan

Design by Wendy Dunbar, Ireland
Printed in China by RACTR Printing & Co, Ltd.

ISBN 978-0-9554097-5-2

www.scenicireland.com